YOU
belong

**BECAUSE GOD IS
WHO HE SAYS HE IS**

STUDY GUIDE

Also By Candace Payne

Laugh It Up
(book, ebook, and audio book)

Defiant Joy
(Bible study guide, DVD, and digital video teaching sessions)

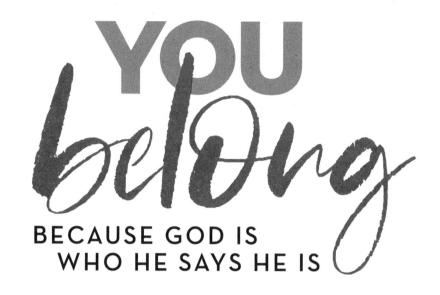

YOU
belong

BECAUSE GOD IS
WHO HE SAYS HE IS

STUDY GUIDE

 SIX SESSIONS

CANDACE PAYNE
WITH DREW TILTON

ZONDERVAN®

You Belong Study Guide

Copyright © 2020 by Candace Payne

ISBN 978-0-310-11332-4 (softcover)

ISBN 978-0-310-11333-1 (ebook)

Requests for information should be addressed to:

Zondervan, 3900 Sparks Dr. SE, Grand Rapids, Michigan 49546

Cover design: Ron Huizinga

Interior design: CrosslinCreative.net

First Printing March 2020 / Printed in the United States of America

Contents

Note from the Author

Hey, ya'll! Candace Payne here. Let me be the first to personally welcome you to the *You Belong* group Bible study. I have found over the years that belonging is one of the deepest desires humans have. Equally, I've found that God also deeply desires for us to understand and experience how we belong to *Him*. Have you ever thought about that?

As I considered this in my own life, I couldn't deny that this intrinsic part of my faith was missing and I went on a journey to uncover it. I read over and over again all these different names describing God. Subsequently, I began to notice that He not only had multiple names for Himself but many descriptors of those who belong to Him as well. I decided to dig into all the names God ascribes to us in our belonging. This allowed me to connect the dots between who He says He is and how we subversively and absolutely belong to Him.

How This Study Guide Works

This study guide contains six guided *Group Gatherings* and six weeks' worth of guided *Fun Work* for you to do on your own in between gatherings. I want to make this study guide easy for you to navigate. So, let's take a closer look at what each of these sections include.

GROUP GATHERINGS

Each gathering is designed to be 70-90 minutes and is divided into three main sections: *Warming Up*, *Press Play*, *Belong Together*. For each session there is also a *Before You Go* section that will help you to prepare for your gathering before you arrive.

Before You Go

This first section is designed as a quick opportunity to prepare your heart and mind for your group gathering *before you arrive*. You can do it before rushing out the door, while eating a quick dinner, or while in your car parked outside of wherever your gathering is being hosted. This is an important opportunity to slow down and open your heart to whatever God might have for you.

Checking In (5 minutes)

Before just diving in each week, make sure you take 5 minutes to check in with one another. This doesn't have to be structured time, but it is important to connect a bit before starting your *Group Gathering* each week.

Press Play (18–22 minutes)

After reading a short introduction, you will start each gathering by watching a video featuring Yours Truly. This will help you to think about how *You Belong* from a different angle each week. Take notes, write down questions, and notice what stands out to you. Each video is about 15 minutes, after which you will have a minute to yourself to write down your initial thoughts.

Belong Together (30–50 minutes)

The bulk of your time together will be spent interacting with each other as you talk through various questions, activities, and Bible verses. Each session will include opportunities to (1) take a quick *Pit Stop* by doing something engaging and interactive together, (2) *Explore the Idea* by talking through the main concept for that week, (3) *Unpack Some Truth* as you take a closer look at a couple passages of Scripture, and (4) go *Off the Beaten Path* by engaging in a group exercise. You will also have a weekly stop at the (5) *Souvenir Shop* as you consider what would be useful to take home with you and how you want to challenge yourself this week. You will finally close your time with the (6) *Prayer of Belonging*, a prayer that you will be praying over each other and yourselves throughout this study.

FILL UP WITH FUN WORK

In between each gathering there are a number of suggested activities, prayer experiences, and Bible passages for you to check out. They will definitely give you a deeper, more fulfilling experience with this study, so they are highly recommended. That being said, I hope they can be a time of refuge for you and not a time of stress. I call it *Fun Work* because that is what it is supposed to be! Just think of them as time with your good friend, Jesus.

PACK YOUR BAGS (LEADER'S GUIDE)

In the back of this book (page 115) there is a short leader's guide for each session. These guides are there to help whomever is leading the Group Gathering to prepare beforehand and make sure everyone has the best experience. If you will be leading this group or a session, be sure to check it out!

Alright, party people! Ready to take the plunge?!? I pray that you would not only connect in belonging with one another but also connect deeply in belonging with the God who made you and loves you. Enjoy the ride!

Session 1

DO I BELONG?

Before You Go to Study

Before your Group Gathering this week, take a few minutes to prepare your heart and mind using the prompts below.

PREP

Belonging is a big deal to us humans. To really be a part of something. To feel truly wanted and accepted. To be connected to others in meaningful ways. We seemingly spend our lives trying to be somebody's something (friend, spouse, parent, idol, leader, mentor, boo, babe). It is no wonder then that to not belong is one of our biggest fears. The terror of this concept leaves us always evaluating where we stand with others. *What do they think of me? How do I fit? Do I really belong?* I believe that the answer is a resounding "Yes!" and, over the course of this study, I hope God shows you just how much!

What are you hoping to see happen in your life during the course of this study? What might God want for you during this time?

> "Your life is not your own: it belongs to God. To 'be yourself' is to be and do what God wants you to be and do, knowing that God created you for a mission and knows you and your mission better than you do."
>
> —Leonard Sweet

Prayer of Belonging

God, I want to know deeply who *You* say You are. In knowing You more fully, I find my identity and belonging in You. As my heart longs to fit in or feel fulfilled, I will trust in *You*. Through the roles You play in my life, the relationship You have with me, and by Your very nature, I understand how I belong to You.

Thank you for paying such a high price to make me Your own. Thank You for being a Father to my orphan heart. Thank You for being my first love. Thank You for creating me with a purpose to live with assignment and authority under Your Son Jesus' leading and instruction. Thank You for shepherding my wandering soul. Thank You for grafting me into Your family and pruning me so that I flourish.

I want to know who You are so intimately that the joy I experience overflows from understanding how I belong to You. And, God, above all, I echo the words Paul wrote in the book of Philippians, chapter 3, verse 12: ". . . I press on to take hold of that for which Christ Jesus took hold of me . . ." I open my heart. Will You open my eyes and ears as well? In Jesus' name, Amen.

Group Gathering

 After spending a few minutes catching up or getting to know each other, select a volunteer to read the following paragraph aloud.

Our world seems to be built around belonging. We create communities, seek out friendships, build families, plan parties, and connect on social media. No matter who you are, something inside you longs to belong. Over the course of this study, we will be exploring together the truth of who and whose you are according to God and what that means for your life. In the process, you will experience that you are God's and He is yours. This study was crafted to help you see, without a doubt, that *You Belong*.

 **(13 minutes)**
Watch the video for Session 1. Feel free to take notes in the space provided.

General Field Notes

You belong to God.

Bible Verses
I Use:

- 1 Corinthians 6:19
- Romans 14:7–9
- John 1:12
- Psalm 103
- Isaiah 41:3
- John 4:4
- 2 Corinthians 1:22
- 2 Corinthians 5:17–19
- Hebrews 12:2
- Luke 9:23–24

Belonging depends on what God has done for you, not what you can do for God.

We do not live as though we belong, because we do not understand how we belong.

Your joy is connected with knowing who God is and how you belong to him.

God is who He says He is and you are His.

"If we have no peace, it is because we have forgotten that we belong to each other."

—Mother Teresa

Slowing Down ❮❮❮❮❮❮❮❮❮

Take a minute to review your notes and write down what stood out to you most during the video. What did you connect with and what challenged you?

Belong  Together

(30–50 minutes)

Use the following questions, Bible passages, and activities to be real with one another, engage in conversation, and connect as a group.

PIT STOP

Supplies Needed: *Bowl of M&Ms or fun-size bag for each person*

Part of feeling like you belong is feeling like you are known. So, this activity is an opportunity to get to know one another a little better. Take a small handful of M&Ms (or one fun-size bag per person) and don't eat any of them. Assign a category for each color, for example:

- Red = family/childhood
- Blue = friends/crazy story
- Yellow = passions/hobbies
- Green = job/school
- Brown = favorite movie/musician/food/dance move

For every one of that color M&M you have, you have to share a fact from that category. (For instance, if you have three yellow M&Ms, you have to share three facts having to do with your passions and hobbies.) Make sure everyone has at least five M&Ms before you start.

EXPLORE THE IDEA

Use the following questions to help your group discuss what was shared in this session's video. Don't be afraid to go "off script" if the conversation is good!

1. What do you think it means to belong in a group, community, or family? How do you see people in the world around you seeking belonging?

2. What stands out for you most about what was covered in this session's video? How does it make you think differently about the importance of belonging?

3. How can exploring the ways we are described by God (His children, sheep, bride, etc.) help us to understand how we belong to God? Which way of belonging to God feels the most difficult for you to accept?

4. How have you seen joy be directly connected to belonging in your life (specifically belonging to God)? How do you want to see your perspective shift when it comes to your sense of belonging in life and where you are seeking it out?

UNPACK SOME TRUTH

Select volunteers to read the following Bible passages aloud and unpack them together. Use the questions provided to help you explore the verses.

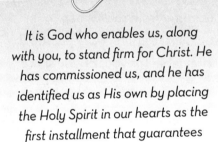

It is God who enables us, along with you, to stand firm for Christ. He has commissioned us, and he has identified us as His own by placing the Holy Spirit in our hearts as the first installment that guarantees everything He has promised us.

2 Corinthians 1:21–22, NLT

- What does it mean to you to know that God identifies you *as His own* in Christ?

- How have you seen others try to earn their belonging to God? How have you tried to do so?

Jesus said to all of his followers, "If you truly desire to be my disciple, you must disown your life completely, embrace my 'cross' as your own, and surrender to my ways. For if you choose self-sacrifice, giving up your lives for my glory, you will embark on a discovery of more and more of true life. But if you choose to keep your lives for yourselves, you will lose what you try to keep.

Luke 9:23–24, TPT

- How can *surrendering to Jesus' ways* and *giving up our lives for his glory* help us to experience true life?

- How is surrender an important step if we are going to accept the true belonging available to us through Jesus? How do you want to surrender to Jesus' way this week?

OFF THE BEATEN PATH

If you have an extra 15–20 minutes, consider engaging in this activity as a group. This is an opportunity to sit in this session's main idea a bit longer and explore it in a creative and intentional way.

As a group, take some time to come up with a definition of *belonging* that is based on what you have learned in this session. Talk about how this definition of belonging is different from your old understanding of belonging. Write your group's new definition of belonging here:

def. *BELONGING:* _____

SOUVENIR SHOP

Draw a picture representing what you want to take home from this Group Gathering. Then write down one challenge you would like to personally pursue this week. Make sure your challenge is stretching yet attainable for you. Briefly share your souvenir and challenge with the group.

My Souvenir:

This week I challenge myself to:

_____

Have your leader or a member of your group read the Prayer of Belonging aloud to close your time together.

Prayer of Belonging

God, we want to know deeply who *You* say You are. In knowing You more fully, we find our identity and belonging in You. As our hearts long to fit in or feel fulfilled, we will trust in *You*. Through the roles You play in our lives, the relationships You have with us, and by Your very nature, we understand how we belong to You.

Thank You for paying such a high price to make us Your own. Thank You for being a Father to our orphan hearts. Thank You for being our first love. Thank You for creating each of us with a purpose to live with assignment and authority under Your Son Jesus' leading and instruction. Thank You for shepherding our wandering souls. Thank You for grafting us into Your family and pruning us so that we flourish.

We want to know who You are so intimately that the joy we experience overflows from understanding how we belong to You. And, God, above all, we echo the words Paul wrote in the book of Philippians, chapter 3, verse 12: ". . . I press on to take hold of that for which Christ Jesus took hold of me. . ." We open our hearts. Will You open our eyes and ears as well? In Jesus' name, Amen.

Filling Up With FUN WORK

As you continue on your journey between gatherings, the following pages are intentionally meant for you to enjoy the content by engaging in activities, prayers, and reading. This isn't academic homework but material that's fully alive and relevant to your daily experience!

THE NAMES WE GO BY

In the space provided, write down names in your life that you accept and respond to. Spend some time with God talking through each name on the list. As you do, write down your reflections. How do you feel when responding to that name? What does it make you feel about who you are? What does it reveal about belonging?

Name	Reflection

Name	Reflection

When you are done, ask God what name (or names) of belonging He wants to highlight for you personally. Listen for a while and write down what He says and how you feel about it.

Name	Reflection

FINDING YOURSELF

In the following word search, find all the names that God gives us as believers. When you are done, pick two or three names that stand out to you the most, look up the verse, and write it in the space provided. Or if you hate word searches, just go straight to picking the God-given names that stand out to you the most!

B	R	E	A	F	B	T	I	M	F	E	R	E	N
G	W	O	N	D	E	R	F	U	L	L	Y	V	E
A	O	C	P	Y	L	O	E	R	T	D	O	L	W
E	R	D	A	T	O	W	S	I	O	N	P	U	C
I	C	A	D	E	V	E	C	B	U	M	T	E	R
N	M	A	S	T	E	R	P	I	E	C	E	D	E
B	E	A	D	A	D	D	E	T	T	O	N	E	A
R	D	S	G	N	A	C	S	E	S	I	R	L	T
A	I	M	E	E	A	D	O	S	Y	F	Z	Y	I
N	O	R	A	R	O	C	E	A	I	O	N	E	O
C	N	E	M	G	R	F	O	U	T	R	E	E	N
H	U	L	I	V	I	N	G	S	T	O	N	E	S
E	C	B	Z	T	E	R	L	O	V	A	P	I	C
S	T	E	R	A	C	H	I	L	D	R	E	N	H

Image of God
(Genesis 1:27)

Branches
(John 15:5)

Wonderfully [Made]
(Psalm 139:13–14)

God's Temple
(1 Corinthians 3:16)

New Creation
(2 Corinthians 5:17)

Beloved
(1 John 4:7)

Free
(Galatians 5:1)

Citizen [in God's Kingdom]
(Philippians 3:20)

Children
(1 John 3:1–2)

Living Stones
(1 Peter 2:5)

Body [of Christ]
(1 Corinthians 12)

Masterpiece
(Ephesians 2:10, NLT)

Write out the names that stood out and the entire verse associated with it in the space below:

Name _____

Scripture

_____

_____

_____

Name _____

Scripture

_____

_____

_____

_____

Name _____

Scripture

_____

_____

_____

_____

> "A deep sense of love and belonging is an irreducible need of all people. We are biologically, cognitively, physically, and spiritually wired to love, to be loved, and to belong. When those needs are not met, we don't function as we were meant to. We break. We fall apart. We numb. We ache. We hurt others. We get sick."
>
> —Brené Brown

Answers can be found in the back of this book on page 129.

TALK TO GOD

Spend some time just talking with God about where you feel like you belong the most and where you feel like you belong the least in your life right now. Tell Him about what you feel, the thoughts you have, and the way you act in response to each situation. Ask Him what He might want to show you about yourself or that situation. If it is helpful, use the space provided below.

Where I Belong Most
Thoughts:

Feelings:

Actions:

God, what do you want to show me?

Where I Belong Least
Thoughts:

Feelings:

Actions:

God, what do you want to show me?

GO THE
mile
EXTRA

For all you overachievers out there, here are some chapters in the Bible that will help you to think more deeply about belonging. If you have some extra time, you should definitely check them out!

Psalm 100

John 10

1 Peter 2

Psalm 139

After you have read each chapter, write down what you learned about belonging to God.

Session 2

THE GOOD SHEPHERD

Before you Go to Study

PREP

A good shepherd guides his or her sheep to what they need in order to receive life and refreshment. In a similar way God uniquely fills and refreshes us. Psalm 23 declares:

The Lord is my shepherd, I lack nothing. He makes me lie down in green pastures, he leads me beside quiet waters, he refreshes my soul. Psalm 23:1–3a, NIV

Sometimes we can resist the green meadows that God offers for our rest and the quiet waters for our refreshment. We wander off in search of this life elsewhere, believing we can find it without God. But the marriages that seem to offer life always leave us wanting. When we trust in the leading and sustenance of God, He declares that we will *lack nothing.*

> "God is alive and faithful to make something beautiful out of us . . . God won't abandon us . . . He's going to replenish it all. He's carrying us in his arms, no matter how bruised or broken we feel."
>
> —Bonnie Gray

Where have you been searching for life outside of God lately? How would you like God to refresh your soul today?

_____

_____

_____

PRAY

This crafted prayer is intended to help you open your heart and mind to God during this study. Pray these words aloud or in your mind as a practice of embracing your belonging.

Prayer of Belonging

God, I want to know deeply who *You* say You are. In knowing You more fully, I find my identity and belonging in You. As my heart longs to fit in or feel fulfilled, I will trust in *You*. Through the roles You play in my life, the relationship You have with me, and by Your very nature, I understand how I belong to You.

Thank you for paying such a high price to make me Your own. Thank You for being a Father to my orphan heart. Thank you for being my first love. Thank You for creating me with a purpose to live with assignment and authority under Your Son Jesus' leading and instruction. Thank You for shepherding my wandering soul. Thank You for grafting me into Your family and pruning me so that I flourish.

I want to know who You are so intimately that the joy I experience overflows from understanding how I belong to You. And, God, above all, I echo the words Paul wrote in the book of Philippians, chapter 3, verse 12: ". . . I press on to take hold of that for which Christ Jesus took hold of me. . . ." I open my heart. Will You open my eyes and ears as well? In Jesus' name, Amen.

GO

Group Gathering

 After spending a few minutes catching up, select a volunteer to read the following paragraph aloud.

One of the most prominent ways in the Bible that God declares His belonging over us is through the analogy of a shepherd's connection to his or her sheep. If you have spent time with domesticated sheep, you know how connected to and dependent they are on their caretaker. God uses this image to demonstrate how He cares for us and how we can trust and depend on Him. Today we will be exploring this idea more in depth and the implications of that relationship has on our lives.

 **(17 minutes)**

Watch the video for Session 2. Feel free to take notes in the space provided.

General Field Notes

You belong to God as a sheep.

Bible Verses I Use:

- John 10:1–18
- Psalm 23
- Luke 15:3–5
- Hebrews 6:1–3

Jesus wants us to follow Him as our Good Shepherd.

Sheep know Provision.

Sheep know Protection.

Sheep know Pursuit.

Sheep know Propitiation.

---

pro·pi·ti·ate | \ prō- pi-shē- āt \ verb

a. to gain or regain the favor or goodwill of [1]
b. to be made right (particularly to God) when you are wrong

---

1   Amended from *Merriam-Webster*. "Propitiate | Definition of Propitiate" Merriam-Webster.com.
    https://www.merriam-webster.com/dictionary/propitiate. (accessed November 18, 2019)

God says you are much more than a "sinner saved by grace."

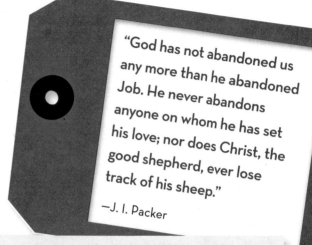

"God has not abandoned us any more than he abandoned Job. He never abandons anyone on whom he has set his love; nor does Christ, the good shepherd, ever lose track of his sheep."

—J. I. Packer

Slowing Down ◄◄◄◄◄◄◄◄◄

Take a minute to review your notes and write down what stood out to you most during the video. What did you connect with and what challenged you?

Belong  Together

(30–50 minutes)

Use the following questions, Bible passages, or activities to be real with one another, engage in conversation, and connect as a group.

PIT STOP

Supplies Needed: *Pens, pencils, colored pencils (optional)*

Set a timer for 7 minutes. In the outline of the sheep below, express to God the state of your heart right now through drawings, words, or a combination of both. Feel free to use as much or as little creativity as you'd like. It is not about being a good artist but about expressing yourself to God in a different way. At the bottom of the page, write a one-sentence prayer about how you need God to be your Shepherd right now. When the timer is finished, have each member of the group briefly share what they drew and the prayer they wrote. If your group is bigger than 6 persons, consider breaking into two or three smaller groups so everyone has a chance to share.

Good Shepherd, I need . . .

Examples: Your sheep can be happy and bright if you are feeling joyful, have a broken leg if you are feeling hurt, surrounded by other sheep if you are feeling taken care of, or living half in the light and half in the dark if you have both good and bad in your life right now.

EXPLORE THE IDEA

Use the following questions to help your group discuss what was shared in this session's video. Don't be afraid to go "off script" if the conversation is good!

1. What is most significant about belonging to God as sheep belong with their shepherd? What do you think Jesus is trying to communicate by describing our relationship this way?

2. What stands out for you most about what was covered in this session's video? How does it make you think differently about the importance of belonging?

3. Which of the four aspects of God's shepherding (provision, protection, pursuit, or propitiation) do you most struggle to believe He will provide? What do think makes that aspect difficult for you to believe and embrace?

4. How might you live differently if you fully believed and embraced that God loved and cared for you as a Good Shepherd cares for His sheep? What could you do to remind yourself of that truth this week?

UNPACK SOME TRUTH

Select volunteers to read the following Bible passages aloud and unpack them together. Use the questions provided to help you explore the verses.

> Now the tax collectors and sinners were all gathering around to hear Jesus. But the Pharisees and the teachers of the law muttered, "This man welcomes sinners and eats with them."
>
> Then Jesus told them this parable: "Suppose one of you has a hundred sheep and loses one of them. Doesn't he leave the ninety-nine in the open country and go after the lost sheep until he finds it? And when he finds it, he joyfully puts it on his shoulders and goes home. Then he calls his friends and neighbors together and says, 'Rejoice with me; I have found my lost sheep.' I tell you that in the same way there will be more rejoicing in heaven over one sinner who repents than over ninety-nine righteous persons who do not need to repent.
>
> **Luke 15:1–7, NIV**

- What do you think is the most powerful part of Jesus' parable of the lost sheep? When have you felt like a lost sheep that Jesus is pursuing?

- What makes us believe that Jesus will not pursue us in our sin? How do you need your Good Shepherd most today?

> Now may the God who brought us peace by raising from the dead our Lord Jesus Christ so that he would be the Great Shepherd of his flock; and by the power of the blood of the eternal covenant may he work perfection into every part of you giving you all that you need to fulfill your destiny. And may he express through you all that is excellent and pleasing to him through your life-union with Jesus the Anointed One who is to receive all glory forever! Amen!
>
> **Hebrews 13:20–21, TPT**

- What part of the verses above stand out to you the most? What do you discover in this passage about the impact that belonging to Jesus has on our lives and hearts?

- What do you think it means that your Great Shepherd will work perfection into every part of you? How can Jesus' shepherding relationship to us help us to fulfill our destiny?

OFF THE BEATEN PATH

If you have an extra 15–20 minutes, consider engaging in this activity as a group. This is an opportunity to sit in this session's main idea a bit longer and explore it in a creative and intentional way.

> "Where does your security lie? Is God your refuge, your hiding place, your stronghold, your shepherd, your counselor, your friend, your redeemer, your savior, your guide? If He is, you don't need to search any further for security."
>
> —Elisabeth Elliot

Activity:

Scripture describes how we are to care for one another as under-shepherds, allowing Jesus, our Chief Shepherd, to work through us:

> Be shepherds of God's flock that is under your care, watching over them—not because you must, but because you are willing, as God wants you to be; not pursuing dishonest gain, but eager to serve; not lording it over those entrusted to you, but being examples to the flock. And when the Chief Shepherd appears, you will receive the crown of glory that will never fade away. 1 Peter 5:2–4, NIV

Using the verse above and what you have learned about shepherding, spend some time talking through the ways that you all hope this group will shepherd one another. These are your group values. Give each value a one- or two-word name and write down a short description explaining why that value is important to the group. Come up with at least five and have everyone write them down in the space provided below.

(Example: *Safety—this is a safe place to be honest without fear of judgment or condemnation.*)

Value	Description
1.	
2.	
3.	
4.	
5.	

SOUVENIR SHOP

Draw a picture representing what you want to take home from this Group Gathering. Then write down one challenge you would like to personally pursue this week. Make sure your challenge is stretching yet attainable for you. Briefly share your souvenir and challenge with the group.

This week I challenge myself to:

Have your leader or a member of your group read the Prayer of Belonging aloud to close your time together.

Prayer of Belonging

God, we want to know deeply who *You* say You are. In knowing You more fully, we find our identity and belonging in You. As our hearts long to fit in or feel fulfilled, we will trust in *You*. Through the roles You play in our lives, the relationships You have with us, and by Your very nature, we understand how we belong to You.

Thank You for paying such a high price to make us Your own. Thank You for being a Father to our orphan hearts. Thank You for being our first love. Thank You for creating each of us with a purpose to live with assignment and authority under Your Son Jesus' leading and instruction. Thank You for shepherding our wandering souls. Thank You for grafting us into Your family and pruning us so that we flourish.

We want to know who You are so intimately that the joy we experience overflows from understanding how we belong to You. And, God, above all, we echo the words Paul wrote in the book of Philippians, chapter 3, verse 12: ". . . I press on to take hold of that for which Christ Jesus took hold of me . . ." We open our hearts. Will You open our eyes and ears as well? In Jesus' name, Amen.

Filling Up With

FUN WORK

As you continue on your journey between gatherings, the following pages are intentionally meant for you to enjoy the content by engaging in activities, prayers, and reading. This isn't academic homework but material that's fully alive and relevant to your daily experience!

FILLING YOUR HEART

Supplies:

- Large bag of cotton balls
- Large clear container (Mason jar or large plastic cup)

Instructions:

- Buy a large bag of cotton balls.
- Find a clear container (such as a Mason jar or large plastic cup). Stick a label on the container with the words: "The Lord is My Shepherd" written on it.

As you go throughout your week, pay attention to where you notice the Good Shepherd's PROTECTION, PROVISION, PROPITIATION, and PURSUIT in your life. How is He inviting you into a place of intimacy?

1. Every time you notice God show up in ANY OF THESE WAYS, put one cotton ball in the container.

2. As you watch that container fill up, reflect on the goodness of your Shepherd and thank Him for how you are known and belong to Him.

> "You have a God who hears you, the power of love behind you, the Holy Spirit within you, and all of heaven ahead of you. If you have the Shepherd, you have grace for every sin, direction for every turn, a candle for every corner and an anchor for every storm. You have everything you need."
>
> —Max Lucado

FRIENDSHIP BRACELET

Using string or wool yarn, make TWO friendship bracelets: one for yourself and one for someone else in need of encouragement.

Try to think of someone who struggles to believe they are protected and provided for by God. Let them know that they belong to a Good Shepherd. Every time you look at your bracelet, remember how Jesus cares for you as the Good Shepherd and ask your friend if they would be willing to do the same. Say a quick prayer for your friend, asking that he or she would experience Jesus as the Good Shepherd every time you look at your bracelet.

*If your friend is really closed off to even a conversation about God, you can just give him or her the bracelet and remember to pray for them.

Braiding a Simple Bracelet

Feel free to use the following guide to braiding a simple friendship bracelet or check online for other more elaborate methods.

1. Cut three strands of your yarn or string about four times the length you want your bracelet. If you want to get a little more creative, put together a fun color pallet by using different color string or yarn for each strand.

2. At one end, tie together all three strands. Leave a little excess string above the knot so you can eventually tie it to the wrist. Tape the knotted end to a table, allowing the three loose ends of the strands to dangle off the edge.

3. Take the strand on the outside left ("A") and weave it over the center strand ("B") and under the strand on the outside right ("C"). Now the strand that was originally on the left ("A") has moved to the outside right.

4. Repeat this pattern next with the "B" strand moving it from the left, over the "C" strand in the center, and under the "A" strand on the right. Next move the "C" strand from left to right in the same weaving motion.

5. Once you have reached your desired length, tie a knot on the other end leaving enough extra string to tie it on to someone's wrist.

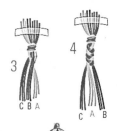

EMBRACING GOD'S TRUTH

Spend some time considering the four ways God is your Shepherd as discussed at your past Group Gathering (Protection, Provision, Propitiation, and Pursuit). Ask God what lies you might be believing about each area. If any lies come up, write them down in the space provided below. When you are done, use the Prayer of Embrace to reject in Jesus' name the lies you are believing and embrace God's truth.

	Lie to Reject	Truth to Embrace	Verse
Protection		I do not need to be afraid because God will never leave or abandon me.	*Be strong and courageous. Do not be afraid or terrified because of them, for the LORD your God goes with you; he will never leave you nor forsake you.* Deuteronomy 31:6, NIV
Provision		God is able to bless me abundantly and will give me all I need.	*And God is able to bless you abundantly, so that in all things at all times, having all that you need, you will abound in every good work.* 2 Corinthians 9:8, NIV
Propitiation		Even when I am powerless, God is powerful enough to save me.	*You see, at just the right time, when we were still powerless, Christ died for the ungodly. Very rarely will anyone die for a righteous person, though for a good person someone might possibly dare to die. But God demonstrates his own love for us in this: While we were still sinners, Christ died for us.* Romans 5:6–8, NIV
Pursuit		No matter how far I stray, God will lovingly pursue me.	*Where can I go from your Spirit? Where can I flee from your presence? If I go up to the heavens, you are there; if I make my bed in the depths, you are there. If I rise on the wings of the dawn, if I settle on the far side of the sea, even there your hand will guide me, your right hand will hold me fast.* Psalm 139:7–10, NIV

pro·pi·ti·ate | \ prō- pi-shē- āt \ verb

a. to gain or regain the favor or goodwill of [2]
b. to be made right (particularly to God) when you are wrong

Prayer of Embrace

Use the chart above to say the following prayer aloud to God. Pray the Prayer of Embrace for each lie that you want to reject.

"Lord, I confess that I have embraced the lie that _____ **(insert lie here)**. I reject this lie in Jesus' name and instead embrace the truth that _____ **(insert corresponding truth)**. Thank you, Lord, and help me to seal this truth in my heart."

For all you overachievers out there, here are some chapters in the Bible that will help you to think more deeply about belonging. If you have some extra time you should definitely check them out!

John 10

1 Peter 5

2   Amended from *Merriam-Webster*. "Propitiate | Definition of Propitiate" Merriam-Webster.com. https://www.merriam-webster.com/dictionary/propitiate. (accessed November 18, 2019)

Luke 15

Hebrews 6

Matthew 9

After you have read each chapter, write down what you learned about belonging to God.

Session 3

THE HEAVENLY FATHER

Before You Go to Study

PREP

Thinking of God as Father can come with a lot of baggage. No matter how good a dad you had, it is impossible for our earthly fathers to represent the perfect fatherly love of God. As a result, thinking of God as our true Father can be a mixed bag of things that express His love well and things that do not. Before you walk into your session, prepare your heart by recognizing what baggage you are bringing with you. Ask God what about His fatherly character you should embrace as true and what you need to let go of as a lie.

Where has God as Father been represented to you well? How have you misunderstood God as Father?

> "Christianity affirms that at the heart of reality is a Heart, a loving Father who works through history for the salvation of His children."
>
> —Martin Luther King Jr.

Prayer of Belonging

God, I want to know deeply who *You* say You are. In knowing You more fully, I find my identity and belonging in You. As my heart longs to fit in or feel fulfilled, I will trust in *You*. Through the roles You play in my life, the relationship You have with me, and by Your very nature, I understand how I belong to You.

Thank you for paying such a high price to make me Your own. Thank You for being a Father to my orphan heart. Thank you for being my first love. Thank You for creating me with a purpose to live with assignment and authority under Your Son Jesus' leading and instruction. Thank You for shepherding my wandering soul. Thank You for grafting me into Your family and pruning me so that I flourish.

I want to know who You are so intimately that the joy I experience overflows from understanding how I belong to You. And, God, above all, I echo the words Paul wrote in the book of Philippians, chapter 3, verse 12: ". . . I press on to take hold of that for which Christ Jesus took hold of me. . . ." I open my heart. Will You open my eyes and ears as well? In Jesus' name, Amen.

GO

Group Gathering

 After spending a few minutes catching up, select a volunteer to read the following paragraph aloud.

Good or bad, we have all seen examples of fathers in the world around us. God intended for this earthly relationship to help us better understand how we belong to Him. Unfortunately, even the best earthly fathers fall short of our heavenly Father's love for and commitment to us. That is why it is important for us to recognize and open to the love of the only one who can demonstrate this kind of love: God. In this session, I want to help you unpack the truth that, in Christ, you belong to God as His loved and cherished child.

(18 minutes)

Watch the video for Session 3. Feel free to take notes in the space provided.

General Field Notes

Bible Verses I Use:

- 1 John 3
- Ephesians 1:5–6
- Galatians 4:6
- Romans 8:14–16
- John 15:9
- Matthew 3:16–17

You belong as a child of God.

We are born with an orphan identity.

God loves you with the same intensity that He loves His Son.

You're God's child, whom He loves and is well pleased.

Your Good Father has given you brothers and sisters.

Gratitude vs. Entitlement

"The child asks of the Father whom he knows. Thus, the essence of Christian prayer is not general adoration, but definite, concrete petition. The right way to approach God is to stretch out our hands and ask of One who we know has the heart of a Father."

—Dietrich Bonhoeffer

Slowing Down

Take a minute to review your notes and write down what stood out to you most during the video. What did you connect with and what challenged you?

Belong Together

(30–50 minutes)

Use the following questions, Bible passages, or activities to be real with one another, engage in conversation, and connect as a group.

PIT STOP

Supplies Needed: *Two bowls or hats, a phone stopwatch, and three slips of paper per person*

Instructions:

- Split your group into two teams. Give each person in both groups three small slips of paper. (If your total group is larger than 10, give everyone just two slips).

- On each slip of paper, have everyone secretly write a character trait that describes your heavenly Father (e.g., "just," "loving," "strong," etc.). Collect the traits of each team together in two separate hats or bowls, then trade bowls with the other team.

- Select one person from each team to be the *Describer.* The rest of that team will be the *Guessers.*

- The *Describer* on your team will attempt to describe each character trait as fast as possible without saying the actual word written on the slip. (They also can't do "rhymes with" or "starts with.") The *Guessers* from that team will then try to guess what character trait is being described. Then switch teams and have the other *Describer* do the same.

- Have a stopwatch ready on someone's phone to see which team can get through all the character traits in their bowl the fastest.

EXPLORE THE IDEA

Use the following questions to help your group discuss what was shared in this session's video. Don't be afraid to go "off script" if the conversation is good!

1. When thinking of the love of a good father, what comes to mind? In what ways have you seen fatherly figures be both good and bad examples of this love?

2. What stands out for you most about what was covered in this session's video? How does it make you think differently about the importance of belonging?

3. What emotions do you feel knowing that God loves you with the same intensity that He loves His Son, Jesus? How do you want to practice living in gratitude of that love rather than entitlement?

4. How have you experienced the love of your Good Father? In what way have you experienced this love through your brothers and sisters in Christ? What makes your love for others so important when considering your belonging to God as His child?

UNPACK SOME TRUTH

Select volunteers to read the following Bible passages aloud and unpack them together. Use the questions provided to help you explore the verses.

> But when the time arrived that was set by God the Father, God sent his Son, born among us of a woman, born under the conditions of the law so that he might redeem those of us who have been kidnapped by the law. Thus we have been set free to experience our rightful heritage. You can tell for sure that you are now fully adopted as his own children because God sent the Spirit of his Son into our lives crying out, "Papa! Father!" Doesn't that privilege of intimate conversation with God make it plain that you are not a slave, but a child? And if you are a child, you're also an heir, with complete access to the inheritance.
>
> **Galatians 4:4–7, The Message**

- What do you think it means that in Christ you have *complete access to the inheritance* right now as one of His children? How can that inheritance change the way we live, think, and approach God?

- How have you seen yourself forget your identity as a son or daughter of God? How might you act differently if you really embraced that identity as God's child and heir?

This is how God showed his love among us: He sent his one and only Son into the world that we might live through him. This is love: not that we loved God, but that he loved us and sent his Son as an atoning sacrifice for our sins. Dear friends, since God so loved us, we also ought to love one another. No one has ever seen God; but if we love one another, God lives in us and his love is made complete in us.

1 John 4:9–12, NIV

- Given the description in this passage, what do you think real love looks like? How can someone love another as God loves?

- What do you think it means that if we love one another, God lives in us and His love is made complete in us? How can our love for others impact the way we are open to receiving love from our heavenly Father?

OFF THE BEATEN PATH

If you have an extra 15–20 minutes, consider engaging in this activity as a group. This is an opportunity to sit in this session's main idea a bit longer and explore it in a creative and intentional way.

Activity:

Supplies Needed: *Pens and sticky notes*

Spend some time encouraging one another as sisters and brothers in Christ. Have each person prayerfully write a word or short phrase of encouragement on a sticky note for each specific person in your group, finishing the sentence "You are . . ." (e.g. "Suzy, you are strong" or "Mick, you are forgiven.") Pray and think through what might specifically encourage that person. Then stick that sticky note to their back. When everyone is done, have someone else read aloud the words and phrases of encouragement from each person's back.

SOUVENIR SHOP

Draw a picture representing what you want to take home from this Group Gathering. Then write down one challenge you would like to personally implement this week. Make sure your challenge is stretching yet attainable for you. Briefly share your souvenir and challenge with the group.

My Souvenir:

This week I challenge myself to:

"I think a father's job, when it's done best, is to get down on both knees, lean over his children's lives, and whisper, 'Where do you want to go?' Every day God invites us on the same kind of adventure. It's not a trip where He sends us a rigid itinerary, He simply invites us. God asks what it is He's made us to love, what it is that captures our attention, what feeds that deep indescribable need of our souls to experience the richness of the world He made. And then, leaning over us, He whispers, 'Let's go do THAT together.'"

—Bob Goff

Have your leader or a member of your group read the Prayer of Belonging aloud to close your time together.

Prayer of Belonging

God, we want to know deeply who *You* say You are. In knowing You more fully, we find our identity and belonging in You. As our hearts long to fit in or feel fulfilled, we will trust in *You*. Through the roles You play in our lives, the relationships You have with us, and by Your very nature, we understand how we belong to You.

Thank You for paying such a high price to make us Your own. Thank You for being a Father to our orphan hearts. Thank You for being our first love. Thank You for creating each of us with a purpose to live with assignment and authority under Your Son Jesus' leading and instruction. Thank You for shepherding our wandering souls. Thank You for grafting us into Your family and pruning us so that we flourish.

We want to know who You are so intimately that the joy we experience overflows from understanding how we belong to You. And, God, above all, we echo the words Paul wrote in the book of Philippians, chapter 3, verse 12: ". . . I press on to take hold of that for which Christ Jesus took hold of me. . ." We open our hearts. Will You open our eyes and ears as well? In Jesus' name, Amen.

Filling Up With FUN WORK

As you continue on your journey between gatherings, the following pages are for you to engage in activities, prayers, and reading. These are intentionally meant for you to enjoy the content and shift your understanding of Bible study from academic homework, to fully alive and relevant to your daily experience!

COUNTING ON LOVE

First John 3:16 says, "This is how we know what love is: Jesus Christ laid down his life for us. And we ought to lay down our lives for our brothers and sisters."

Keep track of every time you experience the love of your heavenly Father this week by coloring in a portion of the hearts below. For every five portions you color (one full heart), do something kind that will show another the love of the Father. Then spend some time thanking God for what He has done for you and talk to Him about what it was like to show another His love.

"Father, Thank You For . . ."

Reflection on Loving Others

"Father, Thank You For . . ."

Reflection on Loving Others

"Father, Thank You For . . ."

Reflection on Loving Others

"Father, Thank You For . . ."

Reflection on Loving Others

"Father, Thank You For . . ."

Reflection on Loving Others

If you need more space, keep a tallying on the extra note pages at the end of this section.

A LOVE TO REMEMBER

Communicating direct and heartfelt gratitude for our brothers and sisters honors the Father:

> *And let us consider how we may spur one another on toward love and good deeds, not giving up meeting together, as some are in the habit of doing, but encouraging one another—and all the more as you see the Day approaching.*
>
> **—Hebrews 10:24–25, NIV**

Think of three or four brothers and sisters in Christ who have been particularly influential in demonstrating God's love of a Father to you. Send each person a text, give them a call, OR mail a handwritten notecard old school-style to express how much they have meant to you and how you see Father God shining through them.

1. _____

2. _____

3. _____

4. _____

A LETTER TO YOUR FATHER

Write an open and honest letter to God expressing how you have experienced Him as Father. Write both what has been a blessing to you and what has been painful or confusing. When you are done, spend some time listening for how God might want to respond to what you have written. Allow your heavenly Father to hold you in all the emotions you experience.

GO THE *mile* EXTRA

For all you overachievers out there, here are some chapters in the Bible that will help you to think more deeply about belonging. If you have some extra time, you should definitely check them out!

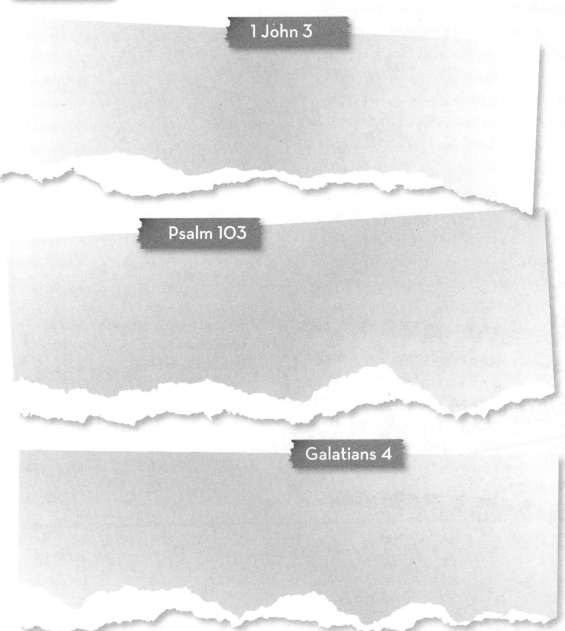

1 John 3

Psalm 103

Galatians 4

John 14

1 John 4

After you have read each chapter, write down what you learned about belonging to God.

"We were never created to settle for mere religion. Jesus did not die so that we could have a religious belief system but rather a life-giving relationship with our Father."

—Christine Caine

Session 4

THE BRIDEGROOM

Before You Go to Study

PREP

One of the ways the Bible describes our belonging to Jesus is through the illustration of a bride and groom. Jesus is the groom who passionately loves us, His bride, and desires that we love Him with the same passion in return. This may seem like an interesting way to think about your relationship with Jesus, but it communicates the level of intimacy God desires with you. As you prepare yourself for this session, think about the intimacy you feel in your relationship with God.

Where do you feel deeply connected with Jesus and where are you holding back?

"To fall in love with God is the greatest romance; to seek him, the greatest adventure; to find him, the greatest human achievement."

—Saint Augustine of Hippo

This crafted prayer is intended to help you open your heart and mind to God during this study. Pray these words aloud or in your mind as a practice of embracing your belonging.

Prayer of Belonging

God, I want to know deeply who *You* say You are. In knowing You more fully, I find my identity and belonging in You. As my heart longs to fit in or feel fulfilled, I will trust in *You*. Through the roles You play in my life, the relationship You have with me, and by Your very nature, I understand how I belong to You.

Thank you for paying such a high price to make me Your own. Thank You for being a Father to my orphan heart. Thank you for being my first love. Thank You for creating me with a purpose to live with assignment and authority under Your Son Jesus' leading and instruction. Thank You for shepherding my wandering soul. Thank You for grafting me into Your family and pruning me so that I flourish.

I want to know who You are so intimately that the joy I experience overflows from understanding how I belong to You. And, God, above all, I echo the words Paul wrote in the book of Philippians, chapter 3, verse 12: ". . . I press on to take hold of that for which Christ Jesus took hold of me. . . ." I open my heart. Will You open my eyes and ears as well? In Jesus' name, Amen.

GO

Group Gathering

 After spending a few minutes catching up, select a volunteer to read the following paragraph aloud.

The greatest level of intimacy is to fully know someone and be fully known by them. This is a level of intimacy Jesus desires to share with each of us individually and all of us together as His Church. It is no wonder then that God describes our belonging to Him in terms of a bride belonging to a bridegroom. He wants to show us that He desires the most intimate of relationships with us. In this session, we will be looking more in depth at what it truly means to be Jesus' bride.

 **(18 minutes)**

Watch the video for Session 4. Feel free to take notes in the space provided.

General Field Notes

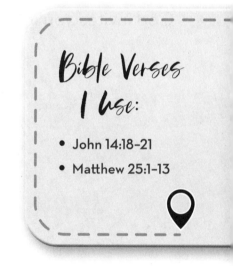

Bible Verses I Use:

- John 14:18–21
- Matthew 25:1–13

We get to have intimacy with Jesus as His bride.

Jesus wants for us to passionately love Him in return.

God invites you into a private and intimate space.

You belong to God even in the waiting.

Others belong to Jesus as His bride too.

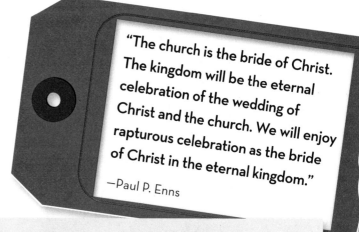

"The church is the bride of Christ. The kingdom will be the eternal celebration of the wedding of Christ and the church. We will enjoy rapturous celebration as the bride of Christ in the eternal kingdom."

—Paul P. Enns

Slowing Down

Take a minute to review your notes and write down what stood out to you most during the video. What did you connect with and what challenged you?

Belong Together

(30–50 minutes)

Use the following questions, Bible passages, and activities to be real with one another, engage in conversation, and connect as a group.

PIT STOP

Supplies Needed: *One bag of marshmallows, one bag of mini marshmallows, a box of toothpicks, and paper plates.*

1. Break into teams of three or four and distribute the toothpicks, marshmallows, and mini marshmallows across each team.

2. Using the supplies, each team tries to create the best-looking marshmallow bride on a paper plate.

3. After five minutes, have each team count how many marshmallows they used to prepare their bride.

4. For every five marshmallows your group uses, write down a way that followers of Jesus can be prepared to encounter their loving heavenly Bridegroom at any moment.

5. After everyone is done, have each team present their bride and discuss what ways of being prepared that they wrote down.

EXPLORE THE IDEA

Use the following questions to help your group discuss what was shared in this session's video. Don't be afraid to go "off script" if the conversation is good!

1. What stands out for you most about what was covered in this session's video? How does it make you think differently about the importance of belonging?

2. How is imagining Jesus as a bridegroom helpful in better understanding how we belong to him? What could it look like to return His love as His bride? How can that mutual love help to create greater intimacy?

3. What do you think it means that you belong to God even in the waiting? Where in your life are you waiting for Jesus right now?

4. What do you think it looks like to be prepared for Jesus' return at all times? How do you personally want to better prepare yourself for your Bridegroom?

UNPACK SOME TRUTH

Read the following Bible passages and unpack them together. Use the questions provided to help you explore the verses.

I pray that out of his glorious riches he may strengthen you with power through his Spirit in your inner being, so that Christ may dwell in your hearts through faith. And I pray that you, being rooted and established in love, may have power, together with all the Lord's holy people, to grasp how wide and long and high and deep is the love of Christ, and to know this love that surpasses knowledge—that you may be filled to the measure of all the fullness of God.

Ephesians 3:16–19, NIV

- What stands out to you about this prayer for intimacy? How does this communicate the powerful love of the Bridegroom?

- What would change if you shared this level of intimacy with God? How do you need God's Spirit to strengthen you in your inner being?

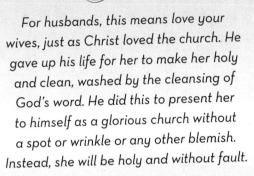

For husbands, this means love your wives, just as Christ loved the church. He gave up his life for her to make her holy and clean, washed by the cleansing of God's word. He did this to present her to himself as a glorious church without a spot or wrinkle or any other blemish. Instead, she will be holy and without fault.

Ephesians 5:25–27, NLT

- What do you learn about Jesus' love for us through the verses above? How does Jesus' love for us prepare us to be His bride?

- What would it look like if, not only husbands but all of us, loved each other as Christ loved the church? How do you want to start giving your life up for others as you interact with them on a daily basis?

OFF THE BEATEN PATH

If you have an extra 15–20 minutes, consider engaging in this activity as a group. This is an opportunity to sit in this session's main idea a bit longer and explore it in a creative and intentional way.

Activity:

This exercise will help you to build intimacy within your group. Break into pairs and sit or stand face-to-face. Set a timer for 2 minutes. One member of each pair will start asking the question, "Who are you?" and the other member will answer by saying the first thing that comes to mind. The first member will repeat the question immediately after each answer for the duration of the timer, while the second person will attempt to answer with continually deeper aspects of who they are. Then switch roles and repeat the process.

When finished, come back together as a group and discuss the experience. What did you learn about your partner, about yourself, and about intimacy? What is it like to know that God wants the deepest level of intimacy with you?

SOUVENIR SHOP

Draw a picture representing what you want to take home from this group gathering. Then write down one challenge you would like to personally implement this week. Make sure your challenge is stretching yet attainable for you. Briefly share your souvenir and challenge with the group.

My Souvenir:

This week I challenge myself to:

"God can take what Satan meant for shame and use it for His glory. Just when we think we've messed up so badly that our lives are nothing but heaps of ashes, God pours His living water over us and mixes the ashes into clay. He then takes this clay and molds it into a vessel of beauty. After He fills us with His overflowing love, He can use us to pour His love into the hurting lives of others."

—Lysa TerKeurst

PRAY

Have your leader or a member of your group read the Prayer of Belonging aloud to close your time together.

Prayer of Belonging

God, we want to know deeply who *You* say You are. In knowing You more fully, we find our identity and belonging in You. As our hearts long to fit in or feel fulfilled, we will trust in *You*. Through the roles You play in our lives, the relationships You have with us, and by Your very nature, we understand how we belong to You.

Thank You for paying such a high price to make us Your own. Thank You for being a Father to our orphan hearts. Thank You for being our first love. Thank You for creating each of us with a purpose to live with assignment and authority under Your Son Jesus' leading and instruction. Thank You for shepherding our wandering souls. Thank You for grafting us into Your family and pruning us so that we flourish.

We want to know who You are so intimately that the joy we experience overflows from understanding how we belong to You. And, God, above all, we echo the words Paul wrote in the book of Philippians, chapter 3, verse 12: ". . . I press on to take hold of that for which Christ Jesus took hold of me. . ." We open our hearts. Will You open our eyes and ears as well? In Jesus' name, Amen.

Filling Up With FUN WORK

As you continue on your journey between gatherings, the following pages are for you to engage and have fun with the content. Feel free to enjoy any or all of these activities, prayers, and readings.

YOUR SUNDAY'S BEST

Each day this week wear your Sunday's Best, whatever that means to you. Every time you are reminded of what you are wearing, be alert and ask Jesus how He wants you to encounter Him in this moment. Think of them as little opportunities to grow in intimacy with your Bridegroom. At the end of each day, write down how you encountered Jesus and how you felt an intimacy with Him.

Day 1:

Day 2:

Day 3:

Day 4:

Day 5:

Day 6:

Day 7:

"If we knew how much God loved us and was for us, we'd talk to Him all day long."

—Donald Miller

SHARING JOY WITH GOD

Find something that is joyful for you and intentionally do it with God. It could be taking a walk together, shooting baskets in the front yard, or working in your garden. Whatever it is, make sure you are able to be present with God in it. Watching TV or scrolling through social media are usually bad choices. When you are done, take some time to journal about the experience.

WORD CROSSED LOVERS

Read the clues to the crossword and discover some biblical truths about God's love. You can look up the passages in the NIV translation of the Bible.

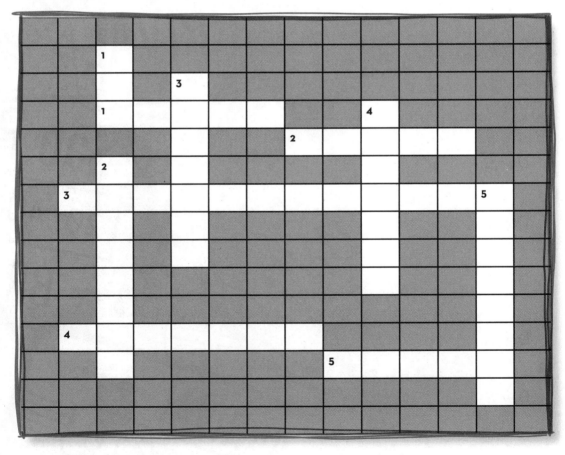

Across

1. For God so loved the _____ that he gave his one and only Son, that whoever believes in him shall not perish but have eternal life. **John 3:16**

2. And now these three remain: _____, hope and love. But the greatest of these is love. **1 Corinthians 13:13**

3. But you, Lord, are a compassionate and gracious God, slow to anger, abounding in love and _____ . **Psalm 86:15**

4. There is no fear in love. But _____ love drives out fear, because fear has to do with punishment. The one who fears is not made perfect in love. **1 John 4:18**

5. Love is patient, love is kind. It does not envy, it does not _____ , it is not proud. **1 Corinthians 13:4**

Down

1. As the Father has loved me, so have I loved you. _____ remain in my love. **John 15:9**

2. See what great love the Father has _____ on us, that we should be called children of God! And that is what we are! The reason the world does not know us is that it did not know him. **1 John 3:1**

3. _____ love has no one than this: to lay down one's life for one's friends. **John 15:13**

4. But God demonstrates his own love for us in this: While we were still _____ , Christ died for us. **Romans 5:8**

5. Neither height nor depth, nor anything else in all creation, will be able to _____ us from the love of God that is in Christ Jesus our Lord. **Romans 8:39**

Answers can be found in the back of this book on page 129.

For all you overachievers out there, here are some chapters in the Bible that will help you to think more deeply about belonging. If you have some extra time, you should definitely check them out!

John 3

Revelation 19

1 Corinthians 13

Psalm 86

John 15

After you have read each chapter, write down what you learned about belonging to God.

Session 5

THE HEAD OF THE BODY

Before You Go to Study

Before your Group Gathering this week, take a few minutes to prepare your heart and mind using the prompts below.

PREP

Did you know that not only do we belong to God, but that we also belong to one another as fellow members of the body of Christ? God has given each of us unique roles and purposes in the body, and we all hold deep value in it. As part of the same body, we find joy when others triumph, and we hurt when others suffer. When we are in touch with Jesus, the Head of the body, He will guide us all to move in sync with one another to accomplish His good purposes in this world.

How have you seen God guide you to move in sync with others to accomplish His good purposes?

> "The temple of God is the holy people in Jesus Christ. The Body of Christ is the living temple of God and of the new humanity."
>
> —Dietrich Bonhoeffer

This crafted prayer is intended to help you open your heart and mind to God during this study. Pray these words aloud or in your mind as a practice of embracing your belonging.

Prayer of Belonging

God, I want to know deeply who *You* say You are. In knowing You more fully, I find my identity and belonging in You. As my heart longs to fit in or feel fulfilled, I will trust in *You.* Through the roles You play in my life, the relationship You have with me, and by Your very nature, I understand how I belong to You.

Thank you for paying such a high price to make me Your own. Thank You for being a Father to my orphan heart. Thank you for being my first love. Thank You for creating me with a purpose to live with assignment and authority under Your Son Jesus' leading and instruction. Thank You for shepherding my wandering soul. Thank You for grafting me into Your family and pruning me so that I flourish.

I want to know who You are so intimately that the joy I experience overflows from understanding how I belong to You. And, God, above all, I echo the words Paul wrote in the book of Philippians, chapter 3, verse 12: ". . . I press on to take hold of that for which Christ Jesus took hold of me. . . ." I open my heart. Will You open my eyes and ears as well? In Jesus' name, Amen.

GO

Group Gathering

After spending a few minutes catching up, select a volunteer to read the following paragraph aloud.

A body, even with all its varying parts, is united. It moves and responds as one all working together. If a certain part is limited the entire body cannot function to its full capacity. When a part of the body hurts, the rest of the body hurts with it. Like the parts of the body, believers are intended to interact with one another in much the same way. We are to move as one, help each other reach our maximum potential, and care for each other as we hurt. In this session we will be looking at how we belong to Christ as His body and belong to each other as fellow members of the church.

(18 minutes)

Watch the video for Session 5. Feel free to take notes in the space provided.

General Field Notes

Bible Verses I Use:

- 1 Corinthians 12:12–27
- Acts 17:26–28
- John 17:9–11

You belong to Christ as a part of His body.

We each have a unique function in the body, and diversity is necessary.

Christ is the head coordinating us to move together in unity.

We confuse unity for uniformity.

When one part of the body suffers, the whole suffers.

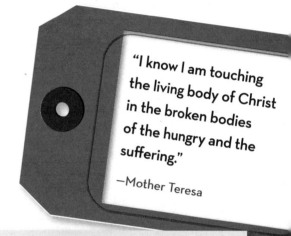

"I know I am touching the living body of Christ in the broken bodies of the hungry and the suffering."

—Mother Teresa

Slowing Down

Take a minute to review your notes and write down what stood out to you most during the video. What did you connect with and what challenged you?

Belong  Together

(30-50 minutes)

Use the following questions, Bible passages, and activities to be real with one another, engage in conversation, and connect as a group.

PIT STOP

Take time to discuss where you see the value in one another. One at a time, go around and encourage each member of your group by having a few people share where they see that person's unique purposes and value in the body of Christ. You could even suggest the part that they might be in the body. (Example: "Lester, you are the hands because you are always serving," or, "Tina, you remind me of an ear because of your incredible listening skills and how you care for me.") Find a place to write their name in the outline of the body at right. If your group is larger than 10, consider breaking into two or three smaller groups.

This is not an opportunity to make jokes, call somebody out, or give a backhanded compliment. (e.g., "Lucille, you would be a mouth because you just can't stop talking.") Be thoughtful and prayerful about your words offering only what is encouraging. Think about your responses as you consider how each member of your group adds to the whole of your group, to the whole of the body. Remember, some parts are more subtle than others and some held more in modesty and are obvious.

EXPLORE THE IDEA

Use the following questions to help your group discuss what was shared in this session's video. Don't be afraid to go "off script" if the conversation is good!

1. What stands out for you most about what was covered in this session's video? How does it make you think differently about the importance of belonging?

2. What is it like to know that we each have unique purposes as a part of the body of Christ? Discuss which parts are less obvious and compare them to the obvious ones. How would you guide someone seeking to better understand their own God-given purpose? Share with your group what you feel your purpose in the body to be.

3. What makes it so important to have constant connection and communication with Christ, the Head of the body? What do you think it means to live, move, and have our being in Him?

4. How is unity different than uniformity? How can we better move in sync with each other and Christ in the midst of our diversity?

UNPACK SOME TRUTH

Select volunteers to read the following Bible passages aloud and unpack them together. Use the questions provided to help you explore the verses.

> Just as our bodies have many parts and each part has a special function, so it is with Christ's body. We are many parts of one body, and we all belong to each other. In his grace, God has given us different gifts for doing certain things well. So if God has given you the ability to prophesy, speak out with as much faith as God has given you. If your gift is serving others, serve them well. If you are a teacher, teach well. If your gift is to encourage others, be encouraging. If it is giving, give generously. If God has given you leadership ability, take the responsibility seriously. And if you have a gift for showing kindness to others, do it gladly.
>
> **Romans 12:4–8, NLT**

- How do we as the Body of Christ all **belong to each other**? How can we as one body belonging to each other better care for each other?

- What makes it so important to recognize how we are uniquely gifted and then lean into that gifting? Who have you seen lean into their gifting well?

But instead we will remain strong and always sincere in our love as we express the truth. All our direction and ministries will flow from Christ and lead us deeper into him, the anointed Head of his body, the church. For his "body" has been formed in his image and is closely joined together and constantly connected as one. And every member has been given divine gifts to contribute to the growth of all; and as these gifts operate effectively throughout the whole body, we are built up and made perfect in love.

Ephesians 4:15–16, TPT

- What do you think it means to have all our direction and ministries . . . flow from Christ? How have you experienced Jesus guiding you as the Head of the body?

- What giftings have you noticed in your own life? How do you want to better operate in your unique role in the body?

OFF THE BEATEN PATH

If you have an extra 15–20 minutes, consider engaging in this activity as a group. This is an opportunity to sit in this session's main idea a bit longer and explore it in a creative and intentional way.

Activity:

As a group, take the time to check in with one another, having everyone answer the question, "Where do I need the support of the body most right now?" After each person has shared, take time to encourage and pray for them. If your group is larger than 10, consider breaking into two or three smaller groups.

SOUVENIR SHOP

Draw a picture representing what you want to take home from this Group Gathering. Then write down one challenge you would like to personally implement this week. Make sure your challenge is stretching yet attainable for you. Briefly share your souvenir and challenge with the group.

My Souvenir:

This week I challenge myself to:

"In whatever way you can do so, according to the talents and gifts God has given you, you are to be salt, and light, and whatever part of the Body of Christ you were made to be. You need to tell us what's going on with you so the rest of the Body (of which you are a part) can work together with you."

—Chris Manion

Have your leader or a member of your group read the Prayer of Belonging aloud to close your time together.

Prayer of Belonging

God, we want to know deeply who *You* say You are. In knowing You more fully, we find our identity and belonging in You. As our hearts long to fit in or feel fulfilled, we will trust in *You*. Through the roles You play in our lives, the relationships You have with us, and by Your very nature, we understand how we belong to You.

Thank You for paying such a high price to make us Your own. Thank You for being a Father to our orphan hearts. Thank You for being our first love. Thank You for creating each of us with a purpose to live with assignment and authority under Your Son Jesus' leading and instruction. Thank You for shepherding our wandering souls. Thank You for grafting us into Your family and pruning us so that we flourish.

We want to know who You are so intimately that the joy we experience overflows from understanding how we belong to You. And, God, above all, we echo the words Paul wrote in the book of Philippians, chapter 3, verse 12: ". . . I press on to take hold of that for which Christ Jesus took hold of me. . ." We open our hearts. Will You open our eyes and ears as well? In Jesus' name, Amen.

Filling Up With FUN WORK

As you continue on your journey between gatherings, the following pages are for you to engage and have fun with the content. Feel free to enjoy any or all of these activities, prayers, and readings.

CARING FOR THE BODY

Do something to care for your body in a special way for seven straight days this week. It could be walking, stretching, taking naps, eating salads, or sitting in the bath. As you do, notice how your body responds and prayerfully ask God to better reveal your unique purposes and deep value to Him in His body. At the end of the week, reflect on the experience and ask God who is someone, a part of the body, that I might be able to help care for this week. Reach out to them and let them know that God has put them on your heart.

Here are a few tests we recommend:

- spiritualgiftstest.com
- giftstest.com
- gifts.churchgrowth.org

LEARNING YOUR GIFTS

Go online to take a spiritual gifts test and see what it reveals. Keep in mind that these online tests can only point you in the right direction and are not a replacement for the ongoing discernment that accompanies prayer, trial and error, and the Spirit-led feedback of those who know you best. When you are done, reflect with God about what you learn.

> "When the body of Christ unites, the enemy will have no one to divide."
>
> —Gift Gugu Mona

LISTENING TO THE HEAD

Spend some time learning to listen in your heart to Christ, the Head of the body. Ask Him how He desires you to live as a part of His body today and spend some time in silence just listening for His answer. He may speak through a word that comes to mind, an impression that He puts on your heart, or a verse that surfaces in your heart. Write down a word or phrase or draw a picture that represents what you heard in the outline of the head at right. When you are done, reflect with God on the experience and write down anything that He may have said to you.

For all you overachievers out there, here are some chapters in the Bible that will help you to think more deeply about belonging. If you have some extra time, you should definitely check them out!

1 Corinthians 12

Colossians 3

Ephesians 2

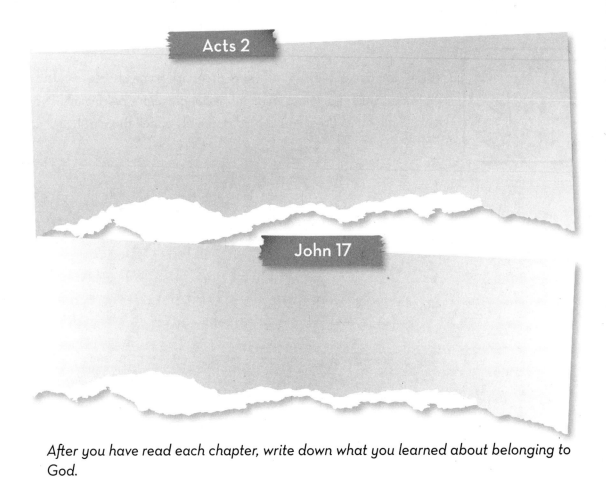

Acts 2

John 17

After you have read each chapter, write down what you learned about belonging to God.

THE SOURCE OF BELONGING

Before You Go to Study

PREP

When the Bible talks about bearing fruit, it is helping us to understand that living alongside God and allowing His good works to flow through us is not about how strong we are. A branch does not work hard or access its own power to bear fruit. The vine transmits its nutrients and water to the branch so that fruit can begin to grow. All the branch is to do is stay open to that connection. In the same way, this is our role with God. If we want to bear fruit that will bring Him glory and join Him in bringing His kingdom here on earth, we need to stay connected to Jesus.

How have you tried to bear fruit on your own? What could it look like to trust in Jesus' power, wisdom, and strength?

> "Abiding in the Vine then comes to be nothing more or less than the restful surrender of the soul to let Christ have all and work all."
>
> —Andrew Murray

This crafted prayer is intended to help you open your heart and mind to God during this study. Pray these words aloud or in your mind as a practice of embracing your belonging.

Prayer of Belonging

God, I want to know deeply who *You* say You are. In knowing You more fully, I find my identity and belonging in You. As my heart longs to fit in or feel fulfilled, I will trust in *You*. Through the roles You play in my life, the relationship You have with me, and by Your very nature, I understand how I belong to You.

Thank you for paying such a high price to make me Your own. Thank You for being a Father to my orphan heart. Thank you for being my first love. Thank You for creating me with a purpose to live with assignment and authority under Your Son Jesus' leading and instruction. Thank You for shepherding my wandering soul. Thank You for grafting me into Your family and pruning me so that I flourish.

I want to know who You are so intimately that the joy I experience overflows from understanding how I belong to You. And, God, above all, I echo the words Paul wrote in the book of Philippians, chapter 3, verse 12: ". . . I press on to take hold of that for which Christ Jesus took hold of me. . . ." I open my heart. Will You open my eyes and ears as well? In Jesus' name, Amen.

GO

Group Gathering

 After spending a few minutes catching up, select a volunteer to read the following paragraph aloud.

So often we approach our lives and faith with will-power and self-sufficiency alone. We act like we are a vine that can grow all by ourselves. God, however, wants us to understand that we are more like a branch. Without staying connected to Jesus who is the true vine, we have no hope of bearing the fruit that God intends us to bear. In this final session, we will take a closer look at how we belong to Jesus as a branch belongs to a vine and explore just how vital our connection to Him really is.

 **(17 minutes)**

Watch the video for Session 6. Feel free to take notes in the space provided.

General Field Notes

We belong to Jesus as branches attached to a vine.

Bible Verses I Use:

- John 15:1–4
- Genesis 1:11–12
- Galatians 5:22–23
- John 14:16–17
- Luke 11:11–13
- Matthew 6:10
- 1 Peter 2:5–10
- John 17:10

You belong in order to bear fruit and multiply.

To bear good fruit we need to allow the Holy Spirit to empower us.

The Holy Spirit is a good gift from your Good Father.

Surrender your life to the vine.

How can I bring God glory through my belonging?

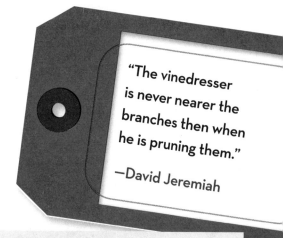

"The vinedresser is never nearer the branches then when he is pruning them."

—David Jeremiah

Slowing Down ⫷⫷⫷⫷⫷⫷

Take a minute to review your notes and write down what stood out to you most during the video. What did you connect with and what challenged you?

Belong  Together

(30–50 minutes)

Use the following questions, Bible passages, and activities to be real with one another, engage in conversation, and connect as a group.

PIT STOP

Take some time to review all you have learned and discussed in the last six sessions by completing the map below. Talk through how these six sessions have helped you to better understand how and why you belong to God.

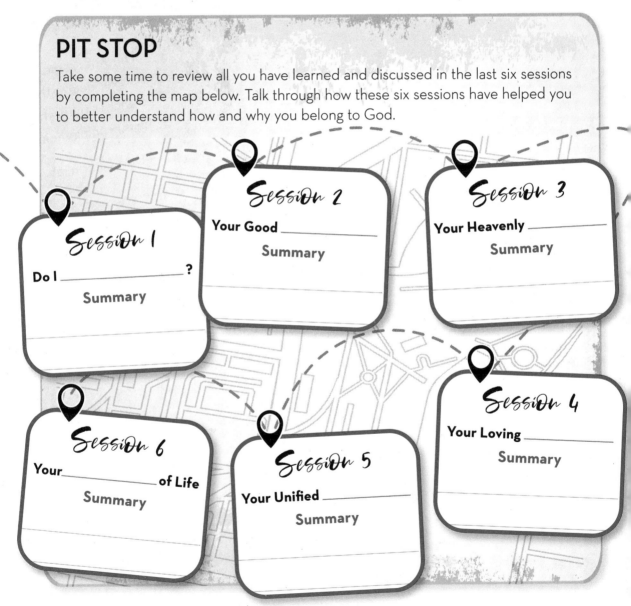

Session 1

Do I _____?

Summary

Session 2

Your Good _____

Summary

Session 3

Your Heavenly _____

Summary

Session 4

Your Loving _____

Summary

Session 5

Your Unified _____

Summary

Session 6

Your _____ of Life

Summary

EXPLORE THE IDEA

Use the following questions to help your group discuss what was shared in this session's video. Don't be afraid to go "off script" if the conversation is good!

1. What stands out for you most about what was covered in this session's video? How does it make you think differently about the importance of belonging?

2. What do you think it means to bear fruit and to multiply? How can we bring God glory by staying attached to Jesus, the Vine?

3. How can someone be empowered by the Holy Spirit? When considering the fruit of the Spirit, what makes the Holy Spirit's empowerment so important?

4. How do you personally want to better surrender to the Vine? How do you think that surrender will shift the way you are living?

UNPACK SOME TRUTH

Select volunteers to read the following Bible passages aloud and unpack them together. Use the questions provided to help you explore the verses.

> I am a true sprouting vine, and the farmer who tends the vine is my Father. He cares for the branches connected to me by lifting and propping up the fruitless branches and pruning every fruitful branch to yield a greater harvest. The words I have spoken over you have already cleansed you. So you must remain in life-union with me, for I remain in life-union with you. For as a branch severed from the vine will not bear fruit, so your life will be fruitless unless you live your life intimately joined to mine.
>
> **John 15:1–4, TPT**

- How can we *remain in life-union* with Jesus? What are some practical ways to pursue this sort of connectedness with the Vine?

- What do you think it looks like to have God prop up the fruitless branches and prune every fruitful branch to yield a greater harvest? How do you see God propping up and pruning you as a branch? How are you bringing God glory with the fruit He is causing you to bear?

The acts of the flesh are obvious: sexual immorality, impurity and debauchery; idolatry and witchcraft; hatred, discord, jealousy, fits of rage, selfish ambition, dissensions, factions and envy; drunkenness, orgies, and the like. I warn you, as I did before, that those who live like this will not inherit the kingdom of God. But the fruit of the Spirit is love, joy, peace, forbearance, kindness, goodness, faithfulness, gentleness and self-control. Against such things there is no law. Those who belong to Christ Jesus have crucified the flesh with its passions and desires. Since we live by the Spirit, let us keep in step with the Spirit.

Galatians 5:19–25, NIV

- How have you seen the world around you live by the flesh? Who have you seen in your life live by the Spirit well?

- What do you think it looks like to keep in step with the Spirit? How can we learn to walk at the Spirit's cadence and rhythm?

OFF THE BEATEN PATH

If you have an extra 15–20 minutes, consider engaging in this activity as a group. This is an opportunity to sit in this session's main idea a bit longer and explore it in a creative and intentional way.

Activity:

Supplies Needed: *Grape juice or wine, bread or crackers, a cup and a plate*

> "Love and Self-control are the bookends of the fruit of the Spirit. Remove one of them and the rest fall over."
>
> —Joyce Meyer

Set up the elements and read aloud together 1 Corinthians 11:23–26. When you are done reading, have everyone take communion together, remembering Christ's death on the cross on our behalf and how He has bonded us together in Him. At the end of your time, pray for your group, thanking God for what He has done in the past six sessions together.

SOUVENIR SHOP

Draw a picture representing what you want to take home from this Group Gathering. Then write down one challenge you would like to personally implement this week. Make sure your challenge is stretching yet attainable for you. Briefly share your souvenir and challenge with the group.

My Souvenir:

This week I challenge myself to:

_____

_____

_____

> "The next sentence is one of the most important spiritual truths you will ever learn: God develops the fruit of the Spirit in your life by allowing you to experience circumstances in which you're tempted to express the exact opposite quality. Character development always involves a choice, and temptation provides that opportunity."
>
> —Rick Warren

Prayer of Belonging

God, we want to know deeply who *You* say You are. In knowing You more fully, we find our identity and belonging in You. As our hearts long to fit in or feel fulfilled, we will trust in *You.* Through the roles You play in our lives, the relationships You have with us, and by Your very nature, we understand how we belong to You.

Thank You for paying such a high price to make us Your own. Thank You for being a Father to our orphan hearts. Thank You for being our first love. Thank You for creating each of us with a purpose to live with assignment and authority under Your Son Jesus' leading and instruction. Thank You for shepherding our wandering souls. Thank You for grafting us into Your family and pruning us so that we flourish.

We want to know who You are so intimately that the joy we experience overflows from understanding how we belong to You. And, God, above all, we echo the words Paul wrote in the book of Philippians, chapter 3, verse 12: ". . . I press on to take hold of that for which Christ Jesus took hold of me. . ." We open our hearts. Will You open our eyes and ears as well? In Jesus' name, Amen.

Filling Up With FUN WORK

As this study comes to a close, the following pages are for you to engage in activities, prayers, and reading. These are intentionally meant for you to enjoy the content and shift your understanding of Bible study from academic homework, to fully alive and relevant to your daily experience!

> *As Jesus and the disciples continued on their way to Jerusalem, they came to a certain village where a woman named Martha welcomed him into her home. Her sister, Mary, sat at the Lord's feet, listening to what he taught. But Martha was distracted by the big dinner she was preparing. She came to Jesus and said, "Lord, doesn't it seem unfair to you that my sister just sits here while I do all the work? Tell her to come and help me." But the Lord said to her, "My dear Martha, you are worried and upset over all these details! There is only one thing worth being concerned about. Mary has discovered it, and it will not be taken away from her."*

Luke 10:38–42, NLT

Spend some time sitting in intentional silence at Jesus' feet. Notice when your heart feels drawn to distraction or worry. Allow those thoughts to drift past as you simply return to your intentional silence with Jesus. Afterward, reflect with God about the experience.

REMAIN BY NUMBER

Spend some time coloring the picture below, using the colors associated with each number. As you do, just relax with Jesus and focus on remaining in Him.

"REMAIN IN ME" —JOHN 15:4

1 = dark green
2 = light green
3 = yellow
4 = dark red
5 = purple

LOOKING BACK

As you wrap up this video study, spend some time talking to God about what you discovered about Him, others, and yourself. Look back through the study guide and notice things that stand out to you. Tell God how your understanding of belonging has shifted over the past six sessions, and ask Him what He wants you to hold tightly to as you conclude.

For all you overachievers out there, here are some chapters in the Bible that will help you to think more deeply about belonging. If you have some extra time, you should definitely check them out!

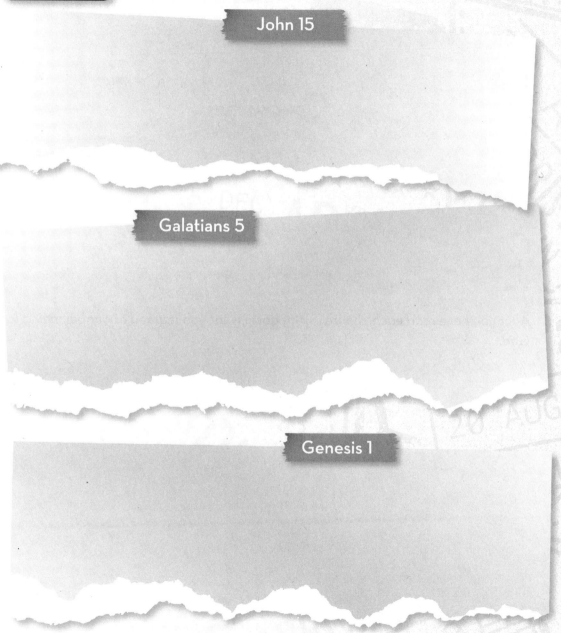

John 15

Galatians 5

Genesis 1

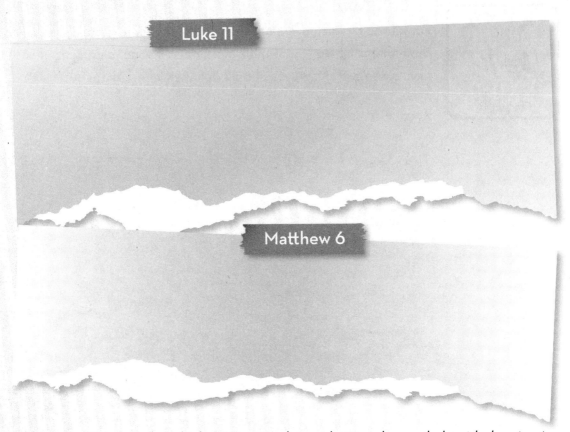

Luke 11

Matthew 6

After you have read each chapter, write down what you learned about belonging to God.

Pack Your Bags

Leader's Guide

1. Do I Belong?

PACK YOUR BAGS (LEADER'S GUIDE)

As the leader of your group or of this week's session, use the following leader's guide to help you prepare and pray that everyone has the best experience.

The Big Idea

Unpacking the importance of belonging and how we belong to God in so many life-shifting ways.

Three Main Points

- Belonging depends on what God has done for you, not what you can do for God.

- Your joy is connected with knowing who God is and how you belong to Him.

- God is who He says He is and you belong to Him

Verses to Check Out

You will unpack the following verses as a group. Read them beforehand to familiarize yourself with what they say and what they teach you about belonging. If you do not have the exact translations, look them up online or read another version.

- *It is God who enables us, along with you, to stand firm for Christ. He has commissioned us, and he has identified us as his own by placing the Holy Spirit in our hearts as the first installment that guarantees everything he has promised us.* **2 Corinthians 1:21–22, NLT**

- *Jesus said to all of his followers, "If you truly desire to be my disciple, you must disown your life completely, embrace my 'cross' as your own, and surrender to my ways. For if you choose self-sacrifice, giving up your lives for my glory, you will embark on a discovery of more and more of true life. But if you choose to keep your lives for yourselves, you will lose what you try to keep."* **Luke 9:23–24, TPT**

Supplies You Will Need

For the *Pit Stop* portion of your *Group Gathering* you will need a bowl of M&Ms or fun-size bag for each person.

How You Can Pray

Spend some time asking God to help your group bond in these early weeks. Pray for connection and belonging among group members and that God would open the hearts of all those who participate.

2. The Good Shepherd

PACK YOUR BAGS (LEADER'S GUIDE)

As the leader of your group or of this week's session, use the following leader's guide to help you prepare and pray that everyone has the best experience.

The Big Idea

Jesus relates to us as a Good Shepherd who is caring for His sheep.

Three Main Points

- Jesus wants us to follow Him as our Good Shepherd.

- Some main ways that Jesus shepherds us is through protection, provision, propitiation, and pursuit.

- God says you are much more than a "sinner saved by grace."

Verses to Check Out

You will unpack the following verses as a group. Read them beforehand to familiarize yourself with what they say and what they teach you about belonging. If you do not have the exact translations, look them up online or read another version.

- *Now the tax collectors and sinners were all gathering around to hear Jesus. But the Pharisees and the teachers of the law muttered, "This man welcomes sinners and eats with them."* **Luke 15:1–7, NIV**

- *Now may the God who brought us peace by raising from the dead our Lord Jesus Christ so that he would be the Great Shepherd of his flock; and by the power of the blood of the eternal covenant may he work perfection into every part of you giving you all that you need to fulfill your destiny. And may he express through you all that is excellent and pleasing to him through your life-union with Jesus the Anointed One who is to receive all glory forever! Amen!* **Hebrews 13:20–21, TPT**

Supplies You Will Need

For the *Pit Stop* portion of your *Group Gathering* you will need pens, pencils, and colored pencils.

How You Can Pray

Spend some time asking God to continue building group unity. Pray that your group would begin to be more open with one another and open to what God wants to do in their hearts. Ask Him to reveal Himself as a Shepherd to the members of your group.

3. The Heavenly Father

PACK YOUR BAGS (LEADER'S GUIDE)

As the leader of your group or of this week's session, use the following leader's guide to help you prepare and pray that everyone has the best experience.

The Big Idea

God loves each of us as a perfect Father and with the same intensity that He loves Christ.

Three Main Points

- We are all born with an orphan identity.

- In Christ, you're God's child, whom He loves and is well pleased.

- Your Good Father has given you brothers and sisters.

Verses to Check Out

You will unpack the following verses as a group. Read them beforehand to familiarize yourself with what they say and what they teach you about belonging. If you do not have the exact translations, look them up online or read another version.

- *But when the time arrived that was set by God the Father, God sent his Son, born among us of a woman, born under the conditions of the law so that he might redeem those of us who have been kidnapped by the law. Thus we have been set free to experience our rightful heritage. You can tell for sure that you are now fully adopted as his own children because God sent the Spirit of his Son into our lives crying out, "Papa! Father!" Doesn't that privilege of intimate conversation with God make it plain that you are not a slave, but a child? And if you are a child, you're also an heir, with complete access to the inheritance.* **Galatians 4:4–7, The Message**

- *This is how God showed his love among us: He sent his one and only Son into the world that we might live through him. This is love: not that we loved God, but that he loved us and sent his Son as an atoning sacrifice for our sins. Dear friends, since God so loved us, we also ought to love one another. No one has ever seen God; but if we love one another, God lives in us and his love is made complete in us.* **1 John 4:9–12, NIV**

Supplies You Will Need

For the *Pit Stop* portion of your *Group Gathering*, you will need two bowls or hats, a phone stopwatch, and three slips of paper per person. For the *Off the Beaten Path* portion of your *Group Gathering*, you will need pens and sticky notes.

How You Can Pray

Spend some time asking God to prepare your group members' hearts to experience Him as Father. Pray that any obstacles to experiencing Him this way would be moved aside and hearts would be open to what God wants to do.

4. The Bridegroom

PACK YOUR BAGS (LEADER'S GUIDE)

As the leader of your group or of this week's session, use the following leader's guide to help you prepare and pray that everyone has the best experience.

The Big Idea

We get to have intimacy with Jesus as His bride, both individually and corporately.

Three Main Points

- Jesus loves us passionately like a bridegroom loves his bride.

- Jesus wants us to passionately love Him in return and invites us into intimacy with Him.

- Others belong to Jesus as His bride too.

Verses to Check Out

You will unpack the following verses as a group. Read them beforehand to familiarize yourself with what they say and what they teach you about belonging. If you do not have the exact translations, look them up online or read another version.

- *I pray that out of his glorious riches he may strengthen you with power through his Spirit in your inner being, so that Christ may dwell in your hearts through faith. And I pray that you, being rooted and established in love, may have power, together with all the Lord's holy people, to grasp how wide and long and high and deep is the love of Christ, and to know this love that surpasses knowledge—that you may be filled to the measure of all the fullness of God.* **Ephesians 3:16–19, NIV**

- *For husbands, this means love your wives, just as Christ loved the church. He gave up his life for her to make her holy and clean, washed by the cleansing of God's word. He did this to present her to himself as a glorious church without a spot or wrinkle or any other blemish. Instead, she will be holy and without fault.* **Ephesians 5:25–27, NLT**

Supplies You Will Need

For the *Pit Stop* portion of your *Group Gathering* you will need one bag of marshmallows, one bag of mini marshmallows, a box of toothpicks, and paper plates.

How You Can Pray

Spend some time asking God to help open the members of your group's hearts to a deeper level of intimacy with Him. Show them the areas that they are holding back from God and soften their hearts so that they can trust Him on deeper and deeper levels.

5. The Head Of The Body

PACK YOUR BAGS (LEADER'S GUIDE)

As the leader of your group or of this week's session, use the following leader's guide to help you prepare and pray that everyone has the best experience.

The Big Idea

We belong to Christ as a part of His diverse body, having unique God-given purposes, roles, and gifts.

Three Main Points

- We each have a unique function in the body, and diversity is necessary.

- Christ is the head, coordinating us to move together in unity.

- When one part of the body suffers, the whole suffers.

Verses to Check Out

You will unpack the following verses as a group. Read them beforehand to familiarize yourself with what they say and what they teach you about belonging. If you do not have the exact translations, look them up online or read another version.

- *Just as our bodies have many parts and each part has a special function, so it is with Christ's body. We are many parts of one body, and we all belong to each other. In his grace, God has given us different gifts for doing certain things well. So if God has given you the ability to prophesy, speak out with as much faith as God has given you. If your gift is serving others, serve them well. If you are a teacher, teach well. If your gift is to encourage others, be encouraging. If it is giving, give generously. If God has given you leadership ability, take the responsibility seriously. And if you have a gift for showing kindness to others, do it gladly.* **Romans 12:4–8, NLT**

- *But instead we will remain strong and always sincere in our love as we express the truth. All our direction and ministries will flow from Christ and lead us deeper into him, the anointed Head of his body, the church. For his "body" has been formed in his image and is closely joined together and constantly connected as one. And every member has been given divine gifts to contribute to the growth of all; and as these gifts operate effectively throughout the whole body, we are built up and made perfect in love.* **Ephesians 4:15-16, TPT**

Supplies You Will Need

You will not need any special supplies for this week's session.

How You Can Pray

Spend some time asking God to reveal to the members of your group their value and purposes as a part of the body of Christ. Ask Him to bring to the surface any way that your group can support one another as fellow members of the same body.

6. The Source Of Belonging

PACK YOUR BAGS (LEADER'S GUIDE)

As the leader of your group or of this week's session, use the following leader's guide to help you prepare and pray that everyone has the best experience.

The Big Idea

We belong to Jesus as branches attached to a vine to bear fruit and multiply.

Three Main Points

- To bear good fruit, we need to stay connected to the vine.

- To bear good fruit, we need to allow the Holy Spirit to empower us.

- The good fruit we bear will bring glory to God and help establish His kingdom on earth.

Verses to Check Out

You will unpack the following verses as a group. Read them beforehand to familiarize yourself with what they say and what they teach you about belonging. If you do not have the exact translations, look them up online or read another version.

- *I am a true sprouting vine, and the farmer who tends the vine is my Father. He cares for the branches connected to me by lifting and propping up the fruitless branches and pruning every fruitful branch to yield a greater harvest. The words I have spoken over you have already cleansed you. So you must remain in life-union with me, for I remain in life-union with you. For as a branch severed from the vine will not bear fruit, so your life will be fruitless unless you live your life intimately joined to mine.* **John 15:1-4, TPT**

- *The acts of the flesh are obvious: sexual immorality, impurity and debauchery; idolatry and witchcraft; hatred, discord, jealousy, fits of rage, selfish ambition, dissensions, factions and envy; drunkenness, orgies, and the like. I warn you, as I did before, that those who live like this will not inherit the kingdom of God. But the fruit of the Spirit is love, joy, peace, forbearance, kindness, goodness, faithfulness, gentleness and self-control. Against such things there is no law. Those who belong to Christ Jesus have crucified the flesh with its passions and desires. Since we live by the Spirit, let us keep in step with the Spirit.* **Galatians 5:19–25, NIV**

Supplies You Will Need

For the *Pit Stop* portion of your *Group Gathering* you will need a grape juice or wine, bread or crackers, and a cup and plate for the communion service; crayons or colored pencils matching the five colors you chose for your key.

How You Can Pray

Spend some time asking God to conclude your group with power, allowing those who are a part of it to see what He has done to transform their hearts and their sense of belonging.

ACTIVITY ANSWER KEY

This is the answer key to the word search found on page 24.

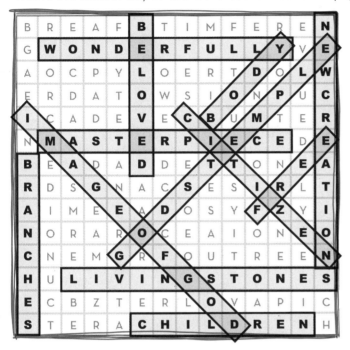

This is the answer key to the crossword found on page 78.

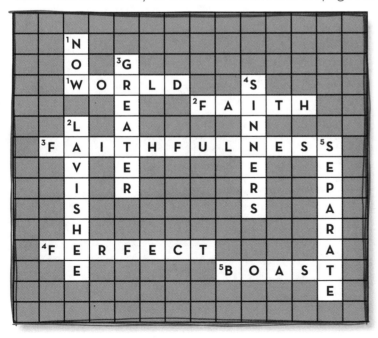

BIBLIOGRAPHY

Session 1

Brown, Brené. *The Gifts of Imperfection: Let Go of Who You Think You're Supposed to Be and Embrace Who You Are*. Center City, MN: Hazelden Publishing, 2010.

McManus, Erwin Raphael. *Soul Cravings: An Exploration of the Human Spirit*. Nashville, TN: Thomas Nelson, 2006.

Mother Teresa, and Brian Kolodiejchuk. *Where There Is Love, There Is God: A Path to Closer Union with God and Greater Love for Others*. New York, NY: Crown Publishing, 2010.

Sweet, Leonard I. *SoulSalsa: 17 Surprising Steps for Godly Living in the 21st Century*. Grand Rapids, MI: Zondervan, 2000.

Youth Group Games. "Mix & Meet" YouthGroupGames.com.au https://youthgroupgames.com.au /games/168/mix-and-meet/ (accessed October 29, 2019).

Session 2

Elliot, Elisabeth. AZQuotes.com. https://www.azquotes.com/quotes/topics/shepherds.html (accessed November 18, 2019).

Gray, Bonnie. *Finding Spiritual Whitespace: Awakening Your Soul to Rest*. Grand Rapids, MI: Revell, 2014.

Lucado, Max. *Traveling Light: Premier Library Edition.* Nashville, TN: Thomas Nelson, 2009.

Merriam-Webster. "Propitiate | Definition of Propitiate" Merriam-Webster.com. https://www. merriam -webster.com/dictionary/propitiate (accessed November 18, 2019).

Packer, J. I. and Carolyn Nystrom. *Knowing God Devotional Journal: A One-Year Guide.* Downers Grove, IL: InterVarsity Press, 2009.

Session 3

Bonhoeffer, Dietrich. *The Cost of Discipleship*. London: SCM Press, 2015.

Caine, Christine. Facebook Post. April 10, 2017. https://www.facebook.com/theChristineCaine/

Goff, Bob. *Love Does*. Nashville, TN: Thomas Nelson, 2014.

King, Jr Martin Luther. *Strength to Love*. New York: Walker and Co., 1981.

Session 4

Augustine of Hippo. AZQuotes.com. https://www.azquotes.com/quotes/topics/intimacy-with-god .html (accessed December 5, 2019).

Enns, Paul P. *Heaven Revealed: What Is It Like? What Will We Do?... And 11 Other Things You've Wondered About*. Chicago, IL: Moody Publishers, 2011.

Miller, Donald. Facebook Post. January 19, 2014. https://www.facebook.com/donaldmillerwords/posts/10151830944541721 .

TerKeurst, Lysa. "Lysa TerKeurst Quotes" Quotes.pub. https://quotes.pub/q/god-can-take-what-satan-meant-for-shame-and-use-it-for-his-g-550836 (accessed December 4, 2019).

Session 5

Bonhoeffer, Dietrich. *The Cost of Discipleship*. London: SCM Press, 2015.

Manion, Chris. *God's Patient Pursuit of My Soul*. Enumclaw, WA: Redemption Press, 2016.

Mona, Gift Gugu. GoodReads.com. https://www.goodreads.com/quotes/tag/body-of-christ (accessed December 7, 2019).

Mother Theresa. GoodReads.com. https://www.goodreads.com/quotes/tag/body-of-christ (accessed December 7, 2019).

Session 6

Jeremiah, David. AZQuotes.com. https://www.azquotes.com/quote/864870 (accessed December 7, 2019).

Meyer, Joyce. AZQuotes.com. https://www.azquotes.com/quote/1069982?ref=fruits-of-the-spirit (accessed December 7, 2019).

Murray, Andrew. *The True Vine*. Chicago: Moody Publishers, 2007.

Warren, Rick. *The Purpose-Driven Life: What on Earth Am I Here For?* Grand Rapids, MI: Zondervan, 2016.

BIBLE STUDY
SOURCE
for women

powered by ChurchSource

Connecting you with the best in

BIBLE STUDY RESOURCES

from many of the world's

MOST TRUSTED BIBLE TEACHERS

| JESS CONNOLLY | JENNIE ALLEN | JADA EDWARDS | CANDACE PAYNE |

Providing

WOMEN'S MINISTRY AND SMALL GROUP LEADERS

with the **INSPIRATION, ENCOURAGEMENT, AND RESOURCES** to grow your ministry

powered by ChurchSource

join our
COMMUNITY

Use our BIBLE STUDY FINDER to quickly find the perfect study for your group,
learn more about all the new studies available, and download FREE printables
to help you make the most of your Bible study experience.

BibleStudySourceForWomen.com

FIND THE *perfect* BIBLE STUDY
for you and your group in 5 MINUTES or LESS!

Find the right study for your women's group
by answering four easy questions:

1. WHAT TYPE OF STUDY DO YOU WANT TO DO?
- *Book of the Bible:* Dive deep into the study of a Bible character, or go through a complete book of the Bible systematically, or add tools to your Bible study methods toolkit.
- *Topical Issues:* Have a need in a specific area of life? Study the Scriptures that pertain to that need. Topics include prayer, joy, purpose, balance, identity in Christ, and more.

2. WHAT LEVEL OF TIME COMMITMENT BETWEEN SESSIONS WOULD YOU LIKE?
- *None:* No personal homework
- *Minimal:* Less than 30 minutes of homework
- *Moderate:* 30 minutes to one hour of homework
- *Substantial:* An hour or more of homework

3. WHAT IS YOUR GROUP'S BIBLE KNOWLEDGE?
- *Beginner:* Group is comprised mostly of women who are new to the Bible or who don't feel confident in their Bible knowledge.
- *Intermediate:* Group has some experience with studying the Bible, and they have some familiarity with the stories in the Bible.
- *Advanced:* Group is comfortable with the Bible, and can handle the challenge of searching the Scriptures for themselves.

4. WHAT FORMAT DO YOU PREFER?
- *Print and Video:* Watch a Bible teacher on video, followed by a facilitated discussion.
- *Print Only:* Have the group leader give a short talk and lead a discussion of a study guide or a book.

Get Started! Plug your answers into the **Bible Study Finder**, and discover the studies that best fit your group!

Check out the Bible Study Finder at:
BibleStudySourcForWomen.com